MANZANITA
SCHOOL LIBRARY
DISCARD
P9-DMO-028

Famous Explorers™

Juan Ponce de León

Claude Hurwicz

The Rosen Publishing Group's
PowerKids Press™
New York

To Amy Hurwicz and Gregory Hurwicz

Published in 2001 by The Rosen Publishing Group, Inc.
29 East 21st Street, New York, NY 10010

Copyright © 2001 by The Rosen Publishing Group, Inc.

All rights reserved. No part of this book may be reproduced in any form without permission in writing from the publisher, except by a reviewer.

Photo Credits: Cover, title page, pp. 4, 7, 11, 20 © North Wind Pictures; pp. 8, 12, 15, 16, 20 © Granger Collection; p. 19 © Archive Photos

First Edition

Book Design: Maria E. Melendez and Felicity Erwin
Layout: Emily Muschinske

Hurwicz, Claude.
    Juan Ponce de León / by Claude Hurwicz.—1st ed.
      p. cm.—(Famous explorers. Set 2)
    Includes index.
    Summary: Briefly describes the life of the Spanish explorer who first came to the New World with Columbus and went on to become governor of Puerto Rico and later came to Florida looking for the Fountain of Youth.
    ISBN 0-8239-5563-X (alk. paper)
    1. Ponce de León, Juan, 1460?–1521—Juvenile literature. 2. Explorers—America—Biography—Juvenile literature. 3. Explorers—Spain—Biography—Juvenile literature. 4. America—Discovery and exploration—Spanish—Juvenile literature. [1. Ponce de León, Juan, 1460?–1521. 2.Explorers. 3. America—Discovery and exploration—Spanish.] I. Title. II. Series.

E125.P7 H87 2000
972.9'02'092—dc21
[B]   00-026965

Manufactured in the United States of America

Contents

Juan Ponce de León

Spain

Juan Ponce de León was born in 1460 during the Age of Exploration. The Age of Exploration lasted from the 1400s to the 1800s. During this time, European rulers sent explorers to claim new lands and bring back riches. Ponce de León was the son of a **noble** family living in León, Spain. Since noble parents educated their children, Ponce de León knew how to read and write. He became a **page** in the royal court. He soon left his position as a page to become a soldier. Ponce de León had a spirit for adventure. This spirit led him to join explorer Christopher Columbus's second **voyage** to the New World.

New World

Explorers from Spain needed permission from King Ferdinand and Queen Isabella before going on a voyage.

5

The Spanish in the New World

The New World included the lands that we now call North, South, and Central America. Some Europeans went to the New World to make new homes and farm the land. Other Europeans went to the New World in search of riches. Ponce de León went to the New World in 1493. He was one of many Spanish soldiers on Christopher Columbus's ship. The mostly Spanish crew sailed to an island called Hispaniola. This island is between the islands that we now call Cuba and Puerto Rico. The men on this voyage wanted to find gold. They wanted the Taino, the Native American group that lived on Hispaniola, to obey them. Ponce de León and the other Spaniards used force to get what they wanted.

Ponce de León traveled to the New World with Columbus. King Ferdinand and Queen Isabella paid for the voyage.

Hispaniola

The Taino and the Spanish

The Taino Indians were skilled artists and house builders. They gathered their food from the plants and ocean. They weren't used to fighting. If they had to fight, they threw stones and used wooden clubs.

The Spanish came to the New World knowing how to fight.. They had swords, shields, knives, armor, cannons, and even an early type of gun called an **arquebus.** They demanded food and gold from the Native Americans. When the Taino and other people of the New World did not obey, the Spanish killed them.

The stones and clubs that the Native Americans fought with were no match for the swords and guns that the Spanish had.

Winning a Battle

Ponce de León helped the Spaniards win a battle against the Taino on the island of Hispaniola. In 1504, Ponce de León was made a **commander** of the Spanish forces in the main city of Hispaniola. This city was called Santo Domingo. The Taino Indians were living in an area east of Santo Domingo. Ponce de León and his soldiers took over this land. They won a battle against the Native Americans and started a **settlement** there. They called the settlement Higuey because that is what the Native Americans had named the area. The Spanish government gave Ponce de León many Native American slaves. He was then made the **lieutenant governor** of the whole eastern side of Hispaniola.

The Spanish destroyed many Native American villages when they came to the New World.

11

12

A Different Kind of Slavery

The Spanish needed help to farm the land and build their houses in the New World. They captured the Native Americans and forced them to work for free. Ponce de León used slaves to build new towns.

Even though Ponce de León was in the New World, he still had to obey the orders of the king and queen of Spain. Ferdinand and Isabella still controlled these newly discovered lands. They did not like the idea of **slavery**. They were happier with something called the *encomienda*. The *encomienda* was similar to slavery. The only difference was that the Spanish had to feed the slaves, clothe them, and teach them Christianity. This system wasn't much better than slavery, in which people had to work for free and were given nothing in return. The Spanish were still very cruel to the Native Americans.

The encomienda *system did not make life any easier for the Native Americans.*

Life in the New World

Ponce de León wanted to find gold in the New World. He also wanted to stay and make a life there. When he became the lieutenant governor of Higuey, he built himself a big house made of stone. He tried to start new towns with farms and families.

Many of Ponce de León's towns did not last very long. A lot of the people who settled in them soon left. They moved on to the places that we now call Panama and Mexico. These people wanted to find gold there. Ponce de León soon left his home in Higuey. Native Americans told him that there was gold on the island now known as Puerto Rico.

This is a map of Puerto Rico from the year 1688. The gold coin is from the time when Queen Isabella and King Ferdinand ruled Spain.

I. DE PTO RICO

ST MARTIN

IST BARTHOLOM

I BARBA

I ST CHRISTOPHLE

NORL

MATATIN
OU
MARTINIQU

15

16

Gold on Puerto Rico

Puerto Rico is an island 70 miles (113 km) to the east of Hispaniola. The Taino who lived on the island called it Borinquen. The Spanish first called it San Juan Bautista, but it later became known as Puerto Rico. Puerto Rico means "rich port" in Spanish. In 1508, Ponce de León went with 200 men to find gold and **colonize** the land. Ponce de León forced the Taino to **mine** the gold that was found. The Spanish government made him governor of Puerto Rico. Before long the Taino who lived on Puerto Rico began fighting the Spanish. The Spanish were taking over their island and making them slaves under the *encomienda* system. With Ponce de León in charge, the Spanish killed most of the Taino on Puerto Rico.

The Spanish forced the Native Americans to mine gold.

The Fountain of Youth

P once de León was told about a Fountain of Youth that was supposed to be on the island of Bimini. This island was north of Puerto Rico. The Fountain of Youth was supposed to be a spring or pool of water that would make a person young again. It was said that a person had to drink the water or bathe in it for its magic to work.

The Fountain of Youth was just a **myth.** After coming to the New World, the Spanish thought anything was possible. Everything in this new land seemed magical. With all the new things being discovered, they thought a Fountain of Youth was possible, too. Ponce de León set out to find the fountain.

Many people believed that the Fountain of Youth really existed. This is what people thought the stream leading to the fountain may have looked like.

From Puerto Rico to Florida

In 1511, Ponce de León was replaced as governor of Puerto Rico by a man named Diego Columbus. Diego was the son of Christopher Columbus. King Ferdinand thought that Diego Columbus deserved to rule the Spanish islands in the New World. Ponce de León decided to explore the lands north of Puerto Rico. On Easter Sunday, Ponce de León and his crew landed on a beautiful coast of what he thought was an island. Ponce de León named this land Florida. Florida means "flower" in Spanish. They did not realize that they had actually reached North America.

Ponce de León and his crew left Florida and went back to Puerto Rico. From Puerto Rico they headed back to Spain.

The top left picture shows Christopher Columbus, his wife, and his two sons. The Spanish began to build settlements in Florida after Ponce de León discovered it for the Europeans (bottom right).

Ponce de León's Last Fight

In 1521, Ponce de León made a second voyage to Florida. He and his men settled there and started to build homes. The Native Americans did not want the Spanish on their land. They attacked Ponce de León and his men when they arrived in Florida. Ponce de León was struck by an arrow and soon died. Today, Ponce de León is remembered as the man who discovered Florida for the Europeans and searched for the Fountain of Youth.

Ponce de León's Timeline

1460-Ponce de León born in Spain.

1493-Ponce de León sails to the New World on Columbus's ship.

1504-Ponce de León and the Spanish take over Hispaniola.

1511-Ponce de León sails to Florida for the first time.

1521-Ponce de León dies.

Glossary

arquebus (AR-kwih-bes) A heavy gun invented in the fifteenth century.

colonize (KAHL-uh-nyz) To settle in a new land and claim it for the government of another country.

commander (kuh-MAN-dur) The person in charge of an army.

encomienda (en-coh-mee-EN-da) The Spanish system of enslaving and converting Native Americans.

lieutenant governor (LOO-teh-nent GUH-vuh-nur) A person who is second in control behind the governor.

mine (MYN) To dig in the earth to find gold.

myth (MITH) A story people make up to explain events in nature or people's history.

noble (NOH-bul) Belonging to royalty or having a high rank.

page (PAYJ) A young boy who serves the king or queen in a royal court.

settlement (SEH-tul-ment) A small village or a group of houses.

slavery (SLAY-ver-ee) The system of one person "owning" another.

voyage (VOY-ij) A journey by water.

Index

Web Sites

To learn more about Ponce de León, check out these Web sites:
http://www.gms.ocps.k12.fl.us/biopage/n-s/deleon.html
http://www.newadvent.org/cathen/12228a.htm